a Day!

Yet another idiot suffering from diarrhea of the mouth and constipation of the brain...

Day 2

INSULT

a Day!

Is your name Laryngitis?
Because you're a pain in the neck...

Day 3

INSULT a Day!

I'll try being nicer if you try being smarter...

Day 4

LAGOON BOOKS

Insult

a Day!

You're a prime candidate for
natural deselection...

LAGOON
BOOKS

Day 5

INSULT a Day!

Don't let your mind wander - it's far too small to be let out on its own...

LAGOON BOOKS

Day 6

INSULT
a Day!

I don't think you are a fool, but what's my opinion compared to that of thousands of others?

Day 7

LAGOON BOOKS

INSULT a Day!

They say that two brains are better than one. In your case, one would have been better than none...

LAGOON BOOKS

Day 8

INSULT
a Day!

If ignorance is bliss, you must be the happiest person alive...

Day 9

LAGOON BOOKS

LAGOON BOOKS

INSULT
a Day!

Do you want people to accept you as you are or do you want them to like you?

Day 10

INSULT

a Day!

He was trying to save both his faces...

John Gunther

Day 11

INSULT

a Day!

Doris: I don't think I've seen you for about ten years.

Boris: Well make the most of it, because with a bit of luck I won't see you for another ten...

Day 12

INSULT

a Day!

I'll bet your father spent the first year
of your life throwing rocks
at the stork...

Irving Brecher

Day 13

INSULT
a Day!

The smallest minds always have
the biggest mouths...

Day 14

INSULT
a Day!

The wheel is still spinning, but the hamster is dead...

LAGOON BOOKS

Day 15

INSULT a Day!

You are cruelly depriving a village of an idiot...

Day 16

LAGOON BOOKS

INSULT
a Day!

If Moses had met you, there would be another commandment...

Day 17

INSULT a Day!

You'd lose an argument with an inanimate object...

LAGOON BOOKS

Day 18

INSULT
a Day!

She was so ugly she could make a mule back away from an oat bin...

Will Rogers

Day 19

INSULT
a Day!

When you go to the mindreader
do you get half price?

LAGOON BOOKS

Day 20

INSULT
a Day!

What happened to your face - do you step on rakes for a hobby?

Day 21

INSULT
a Day!

You're a pork pie short of a picnic...

Day 22

INSULT a Day!

He had a big head and a face so ugly it became almost fascinating...

Ayn Rand

Day 23

LAGOON BOOKS

INSULT

a Day!

You're very open-minded - is that how your brain slipped out?

Day 24

INSULT
a Day!

You're pretty ugly, but beauty is only a light switch away...

LAGOON BOOKS

Day 25

INSULT
a Day!

I like the material of your dress - you were lucky to get so much of it...

Day 26

INSULT
a Day!

Is that your face or did your neck throw up?

Day 27

LAGOON BOOKS

INSULT
a Day!

Are your parents cousins?

Day 28

LAGOON
BOOKS

a Day!

I can hardly contain my indifference...

LAGOON BOOKS

Day 29

LAGOON BOOKS

INSULT a Day!

You're about as sharp as a beach ball...

Day 30

INSULT
a Day!

Talking to you is like talking to a speed bump...

Day 31

LAGOON BOOKS

INSULT
a Day!

I'm busy now, can I ignore you some other time?

Day 32

LAGOON BOOKS

INSULT
a Day!

He hath half a face...

Shakespeare

Day 33

Insult a Day!

Roses are red, violets are blue, I once thought I was ugly, until I saw you...

Day 34

INSULT
a Day!

You have a nasty speech impediment -
your foot...

Day 35

INSULT

a Day!

Do they ever shut up on your planet?

Day 36

INSULT a Day!

Don't you need a license to be that ugly?

LAGOON BOOKS

Day 37

INSULT a Day!

Does Barry Manilow know that you raided his wardrobe?

Day 38

LAGOON BOOKS

INSULT
a Day!

I missed you this time. I'll aim better
next time...

Day 39

INSULT

a Day!

Have a nice day... somewhere else...

Day 40

LAGOON BOOKS

INSULT a Day!

You are so dishonest, I can't even be sure that what you tell me are lies...

LAGOON BOOKS

Day 41

INSULT
a Day!

I'd rather pass a kidney stone than another minute with you...

LAGOON BOOKS

Day 42

LAGOON
BOOKS

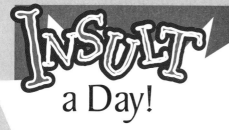

INSULT
a Day!

Thou sodden-witted Lord...

Shakespeare

Day 43

INSULT a Day!

You're so dumb, you couldn't pour water out of a boot even with instructions on the heel...

Day 44

INSULT
a Day!

I'd follow you anywhere, but only out of morbid curiosity...

Day 45

INSULT
a Day!

I like you, people say I have no taste,
but I like you...

Day 46

LAGOON BOOKS

INSULT
a Day!

Fat? You're not fat, you're just -
oh hell, OK.
You are fat. Very fat indeed, in fact...

Day 47

LAGOON BOOKS

INSULT
a Day!

You're so old you can remember when the Dead Sea was just ill...

Day 48

INSULT
a Day!

Thou crusty batch of nature...

Shakespeare

LAGOON BOOKS

Day 49

INSULT
a Day!

I didn't know the circus was in town...

Day 50

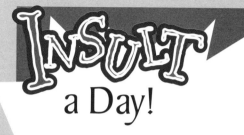

INSULT
a Day!

What do you want to do if you grow up...

LAGOON BOOKS

Day 51

INSULT a Day!

You're about as welcome as a diarrhea in a spacesuit...

Day 52

LAGOON BOOKS

INSULT a Day!

You're so fat, when you get into an elevator, it HAS to go down!

LAGOON BOOKS

Day 53

INSULT
a Day!

Are those your own feet or are you
breaking them in for a clown?

Day 54

LAGOON BOOKS

INSULT

a Day!

Degenerate and base art thou.

Shakespeare

Day 55

INSULT
a Day!

There's nothing wrong with you that
reincarnation won't cure...

Jack E. Leonard

Day 56

INSULT
a Day!

You've got a smile like a crocodile with gas...

Day 57

LAGOON BOOKS

a Day!

You were such an ugly kid, your mum had to tie a steak round your neck to get the puppy to play with you...

Day 58

a Day!

You've got armpits like a pair of
Davy Crockett hats...

Day 59

LAGOON
BOOKS

INSULT
a Day!

Are they shoes on your feet, or the boxes that they came in?

Day 60

INSULT
a Day!

You've got a body like a sock
full of golf balls...

Day 61

LAGOON BOOKS

INSULT
a Day!

If you ever become a mother, can I have one of the puppies?

Charles Pierce

LAGOON BOOKS

Day 63

INSULT
a Day!

I thought of you today. I was in the zoo...

Day 64

LAGOON BOOKS

INSULT a Day!

You can park a bus in the shadow of your behind...

Day 66

INSULT
a Day!

Your conversation is about as interesting as watching a scab form...

Day 67

INSULT
a Day!

Miss United Dairies herself...

David Niven, on Jayne Mansfield

Day 69

LAGOON BOOKS

INSULT

a Day!

Why do you sit there looking like an envelope without any address on it?

Mark Twain

Day 70

INSULT a Day!

I can see that you are flirting with intelligence but getting the cold shoulder in return...

LAGOON BOOKS

Day 71

INSULT a Day!

Please give that face back to the gorilla...

Day 72

INSULT a Day!

If you don't want to give people a bad name, you will have to have your children illegitimately...

Day 73

INSULT a Day!

Anyone who told you to be yourself couldn't have given you worse advice...

LAGOON BOOKS

Day 74

INSULT a Day!

She got her good looks from her father. He's a plastic surgeon...

Groucho Marx

Day 75

LAGOON BOOKS

INSULT a Day!

I see you were so impressed with your first chin that you added two more...

Day 76

LAGOON BOOKS

INSULT

a Day!

You should learn from your parents' mistakes - get sterilized now!

Day 77

INSULT
a Day!

You have an inferiority complex and it's completely justified...

Day 78

LAGOON BOOKS

INSULT
a Day!

That's what they mean by dark and handsome. When it's dark, you're handsome...

Day 79

INSULT
a Day!

Some people say you're two faced, but I disagree. If you had two faces, why would you wear that one?

Day 80

INSULT a Day!

You are starting to sound reasonable.
It's time to increase my medication!

Day 81

INSULT
a Day!

Do thou amend thy face, and I'll amend my life...

Shakespeare

Day 82

LAGOON BOOKS

INSULT
a Day!

Boy: You're most beautiful looking
person I've ever seen.
Girl: So what makes you think I would
want to talk to you, then?

Day 83

INSULT
a Day!

I'm sorry honey, I just don't have the energy to fake it tonight...

Day 84

LAGOON BOOKS

INSULT a Day!

You've got a face like a bulldog chewing a wasp...

Day 85

LAGOON BOOKS

INSULT a Day!

I'm not going deaf. I'm ignoring you...

Day 86

INSULT
a Day!

Bill: Do you kiss with your eyes closed?
Jill: I would if I were kissing you...

Day 87

LAGOON BOOKS

INSULT a Day!

That woman speaks eight languages and can't say 'no' in any of them...

Dorothy Parker

LAGOON BOOKS

Day 88

INSULT a Day!

I can see your point, but I still think you're full of rubbish...

Day 89

LAGOON BOOKS

INSULT
a Day!

You think you're out of this world - and everyone wishes you were...

LAGOON BOOKS

Day 90

INSULT a Day!

If you can't live without me, why aren't you dead already?

Cynthia Heimel

Day 91

INSULT
a Day!

You're not yourself today, I noticed the improvement immediately...

Day 92

LAGOON BOOKS

INSULT
a Day!

You remind me of the ocean - you
make me feel sick...

Day 93

LAGOON BOOKS

INSULT

a Day!

How can you love nature, when it did that to you?

Day 94

LAGOON BOOKS

INSULT a Day!

You can take or leave other people,
after you take from them
you leave them...

LAGOON BOOKS

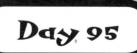

Day 95

INSULT a Day!

LAGOON BOOKS

Some cause happiness wherever they go; others whenever they go...

Oscar Wilde

Day 97

INSULT a Day!

LAGOON BOOKS

They say that travel broadens oneself.
You're so fat, you must have been
around the world...

Day 98

INSULT a Day!

LAGOON BOOKS

You must be the arithmetic man - you add trouble, subtract pleasure, divide attention, and multiply ignorance...

Day 99

INSULT

a Day!

You have no trouble making ends
meet. Your foot is always
in your mouth!

Day 100

LAGOON BOOKS

INSULT a Day!

You're so stupid you would take a ruler to bed to see how long you slept...

LAGOON BOOKS

Day 101

INSULT
a Day!

Only dull people are brilliant
at breakfast...

Oscar Wilde

LAGOON BOOKS

Day 102

INSULT a Day!

They offer counselling for
people like you...

LAGOON BOOKS

Day 103

INSULT a Day!

You owe me a drink: you're so ugly I dropped my glass when I saw you...

Day 104

LAGOON BOOKS

INSULT a Day!

More of your conversation would
infect my brain...

Shakespeare

Day 105

LAGOON
BOOKS

INSULT a Day!

Your shortcomings are self-evident:
I'm not going to point them
out for you...

Day 106

LAGOON
BOOKS

INSULT a Day!

Someday you'll go too far -
and I hope you stay there...

Day 108

LAGOON
BOOKS

INSULT
a Day!

I'll never forget the first time we met - although I'll keep trying...

Day 109

INSULT
a Day!

Sorry if I'm drooling, but I had to get
drunk before I could come
and talk to you...

Day 110

INSULT a Day!

No one can have a higher opinion of him than I have; and I think he's a dirty little beast..

W. S. Gilbert

Day 111

LAGOON BOOKS

INSULT a Day!

Have you been chasing parked cars?

Day 113

LAGOON BOOKS

INSULT a Day!

Trevor: Can you see me in your future?
Tracy: No. You're already in my past...

Day 114

INSULT a Day!

You had an accident at work today -
you were struck by a thought!

LAGOON BOOKS

Day 115

INSULT
a Day!

Whatever kind of look you were
going for, you missed...

LAGOON BOOKS

Day 117

INSULT a Day!

I was seeking for a fool when I found you...

Shakespeare

LAGOON BOOKS

Day 118

INSULT
a Day!

Boris: I've been given a couple of tickets
for the play on Thursday -
do you want to go?
Doris: Only if you give me both of
them...

Day 119

LAGOON
BOOKS

Fred: I know how to please a woman.
Freida: Then please leave me alone.

Day 120

INSULT a Day!

What you look for in a man
is fiscal fitness...

LAGOON
BOOKS

Day 121

INSULT

a Day!

One hell of an outlay for very small return...
Glenda Jackson on men

Day 122

INSULT
a Day!

I bet when you go to the zoo you have to buy two tickets: one to get in and another to get out...

Day 123

a Day!

Haven't I seen your face before - on a police poster?

Day 124

INSULT
a Day!

Do you know what would make you look really good? DISTANCE!

Day 125

INSULT
a Day!

Doris: I can tell that you want me.
Boris: You're so right, I want you to go away.

Day 126

INSULT

a Day!

He has all the virtues I dislike and
none of the vices I admire...

Winston Churchill

Day 127

INSULT a Day!

The only time you don't look in the mirror is when you're backing into a parking place...

Day 128

INSULT
a Day!

You have a waterproof voice.
No one can drown it out...

Day 129

LAGOON BOOKS

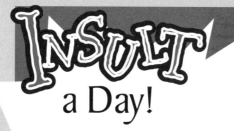

INSULT
a Day!

You're like a Christmas tie - loud and useless...

Day 130

INSULT a Day!

Jack: I want to give myself to you.
Jill: Sorry I don't accept cheap, nasty gifts...

Day 131

LAGOON BOOKS

INSULT
a Day!

You're a nice guy - a nice guy to stay away from!

Day 132

INSULT

a Day!

You're a man of few words. Trouble is,
you keep repeating them...

Day 133

LAGOON
BOOKS

INSULT
a Day!

You get carried away with your own self-importance. The trouble is, you don't get carried far enough away...

Day 134

INSULT a Day!

He has occasional flashes of silence,
which make his conversation
perfectly delightful...

Day 135

LAGOON
BOOKS

INSULT
a Day!

I married your mother because I wanted children; imagine my disappointment when you came along.

Groucho Marx

Day 136

INSULT a Day!

I'd like to run into you again -
sometime when I'm driving and
you're walking...

Day 137

INSULT
a Day!

You may get married someday. You're
waiting for the right amount
to come along...

Day 138

INSULT a Day!

Brian: I would go to the end of the world for you.

Betty: Good, will you stay there too?

Day 139

INSULT
a Day!

Who gave you that tie? Is somebody angry with you?

Day 140

LAGOON BOOKS

INSULT
a Day!

You would never be able to live up to
your reputation, but I see you're
doing your best...

Day 141

a Day!

You are not as bad as they say...you are much, much worse...

Day 142

INSULT a Day!

Save your breath for your inflatable girlfriend...

LAGOON BOOKS

Day 143

INSULT
a Day!

Please call me some day, so I can hang up on you...

Day 144

a Day!

She is a peacock in everything
but beauty...

Oscar Wilde

Day 145

INSULT
a Day!

What fools these mortals be...
Seneca (Moral essays)

Day 146

INSULT a Day!

This is an excellent time to become a missing person...

Day 147

LAGOON BOOKS

INSULT a Day!

I've seen people like you before -
but I had to pay admission...

LAGOON
BOOKS

Day 148

INSULT
a Day!

LAGOON
BOOKS

Annie: Haven't I seen you somewhere before?

Andy: Yeah, that's why I don't go there anymore...

Day 149

INSULT
a Day!

Hey, I remember you when you
only had one stomach...

Day 150

INSULT
a Day!

It's not too hard to find you. Just open my wallet, and there you are!

Day 151

INSULT a Day!

You light up a room...when you leave it...

Day 152

INSULT
a Day!

He's a disease that must be cut away...

Shakespeare

Day 153

INSULT
a Day!

You have a face only a mother could love - and even she hates it...

LAGOON BOOKS

Day 154

a Day!

What you need is a personality transplant...

Day 155

INSULT a Day!

She not only expects the worst, but makes the worst out of it when it happens...

Michael Arlen

Day 156

LAGOON
BOOKS

Insult a Day!

Unless you have something funny to
say, shut your face...

Day 157

LAGOON
BOOKS

INSULT

a Day!

You really are as pretty as a picture,
I'd love to hang you...

Day 158

INSULT

a Day!

Women are like elephants to me: I like to look at them but I wouldn't want to own one...

W C Fields

LAGOON BOOKS

Day 159

INSULT a Day!

You are not obnoxious like so many other people - you are obnoxious in a completely and far worse way...

Day 160

INSULT

a Day!

He smelled as if he had just eaten a
mustard-coated camel...
Martin Amis, London Fields

Day 161

LAGOON BOOKS

INSULT
a Day!

The only man you'll go out with is one who is tall, dark and has some...

LAGOON
BOOKS

Day 162

INSULT
a Day!

She is a waste of makeup...

Day 163

LAGOON
BOOKS

INSULT a Day!

Must you be a pothole in the highway of life?

Day 164

LAGOON BOOKS

INSULT a Day!

You're ugly, I'm busy. Have a nice day...

Day 165

LAGOON BOOKS

LAGOON BOOKS

INSULT
a Day!

There are only two things I dislike
about you - your two faces...

Day 166

INSULT
a Day!

You're a habit I'd like to kick -
with both feet...

Day 167

LAGOON BOOKS

INSULT a Day!

I don't mind you talking so much, as long as you don't mind me not listening...

LAGOON BOOKS

Day 168

INSULT a Day!

He had a winning smile, but everything else was a loser...

George C. Scott

Day 169

LAGOON BOOKS

INSULT
a Day!

He dances like a drunk killing
cockroaches...
John Barbour

Day 170

INSULT
a Day!

Farewell, sour annoy!

Shakespeare

Day 171

a Day!

Ever since I saw you in your family tree,
I've wanted to cut it down...

Day 172

LAGOON BOOKS

INSULT a Day!

As an outsider, what do you think of the human race?

LAGOON BOOKS

Day 173

INSULT

a Day!

Peace, ye fat-guts!

Shakespeare

LAGOON
BOOKS

Day 174

INSULT
a Day!

If I had you for a friend, I wouldn't need any enemies...

Day 175

INSULT a Day!

You use your friends as a drawing account, but you neglect to make deposits...

Day 176

INSULT
a Day!

If you ever need a friend, you will have to buy a dog...

Day 177

LAGOON BOOKS

INSULT

a Day!

Your means are very slender, and
your waste is great...

Shakespeare

Day 178

INSULT a Day!

Phil: Is this seat empty?
Jill: Yes, and this one will be too
if you sit down.

Day 179

LAGOON BOOKS

INSULT a Day!

If I throw a stick, will you leave?

Day 180

INSULT
a Day!

A half-wit gave you a piece of his mind,
and you held on to it...

Day 181

INSULT a Day!

And which dwarf are you?

Day 182

LAGOON BOOKS

INSULT a Day!

Now I know why some animals eat their young...

Day 183

INSULT
a Day!

You're nobody's fool. Let's see if we can get someone to adopt you...

Day 184

LAGOON BOOKS

INSULT a Day!

Sir, as I told you, her beauty and her brain do not go together...

Shakespeare

Day 185

INSULT a Day!

The next time you shave, could you stand an inch or two closer to the razor please?

Day 186

INSULT a Day!

You say no woman ever made a fool out of you. So who did?

Day 187

LAGOON BOOKS

INSULT
a Day!

You do not mind whose means
you live beyond...

Day 188

LAGOON
BOOKS

INSULT a Day!

You're very smart. You have brains you've never used...

Day 190

LAGOON BOOKS

INSULT
a Day!

I would ask you how old you are, but I reckon you can't count that high...

Day 191

INSULT
a Day!

Why, thou dish of fool.

Shakespeare

Day 192

LAGOON BOOKS

INSULT
a Day!

Sorry, I was just trying to imagine you with a personality...

Day 194

LAGOON BOOKS

INSULT a Day!

I see you've set aside this special time to humiliate yourself...

Day 195

INSULT
a Day!

You are so fat you have the only car in town with stretch marks...

Day 196

INSULT a Day!

She has stopped exercising - pushing fifty is enough exercise for her...

Day 197

LAGOON BOOKS

INSULT a Day!

You must have a low opinion of people
if you think they're your equals...

Day 198

INSULT a Day!

Boris: I've come from another planet to seek out beautiful life forms.
Doris: Is that because your race is so ugly?

Day 199

INSULT a Day!

What have we here? A man or a fish?
Dead or alive?

Shakespeare

Day 201

INSULT a Day!

You say that you are always bright
and early. Well, OK, we know
you are early...

Day 202

INSULT a Day!

Someday we'll look back on this, laugh nervously and change the subject...

Day 203

INSULT
a Day!

She does not have an enemy in the world, she's outlived them all...

LAGOON BOOKS

Day 204

INSULT a Day!

You have a lot of well-wishers.
They all wish they could throw you
down one...

Day 205

INSULT a Day!

So, a thought crossed your mind did it?
Must have been a long
and lonely journey...

Day 206

LAGOON BOOKS

INSULT
a Day!

If you were any more vacuous your head would implode...

LAGOON BOOKS

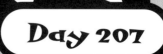

Day 207

INSULT
a Day!

Your best feature is your
ornamental pond...

Day 208

LAGOON
BOOKS

INSULT a Day!

Does your head whistle
in a cross wind?

LAGOON BOOKS

Day 209

Hmm, looks like someone forgot to pay their brain bill...

INSULT a Day!

LAGOON BOOKS

When he is best, he is little worse than a man, and when he is worst, he is little better than a beast...

Shakespeare

Day 211

INSULT a Day!

People clap when they see you
(their hands over their eyes or ears)...

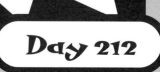

Day 212

INSULT
a Day!

You make me believe in reincarnation.
Nobody can be as stupid as you in
just one lifetime...

LAGOON BOOKS

Day 213

INSULT

a Day!

When you die, I'd like to go to your funeral, but I'll probably have to go to work that day. I believe in business before pleasure...

Day 214

LAGOON BOOKS

INSULT a Day!

Thank you. We're all refreshed and challenged by your unique point of view...

Day 215

INSULT
a Day!

You are master in your own house - the doghouse!

Day 216

LAGOON BOOKS

INSULT a Day!

His garments are rich, but he wears them not handsomely...

Shakespeare

Day 217

LAGOON BOOKS

INSULT a Day!

You got in the gene pool when the lifeguard wasn't watching...

Day 218

LAGOON BOOKS

INSULT

a Day!

You're so fat, it's easier to jump over you than go around...

Day 220

INSULT
a Day!

I used to think that you were a big pain in the neck. Now I have a much lower opinion of you...

Day 221

INSULT a Day!

Some people are has-beens.
You are a never-was...

Day 222

LAGOON BOOKS

INSULT
a Day!

You are so boring that you can't even entertain a doubt...

Day 223

INSULT a Day!

Debating against him is no fun, say something insulting and he looks at you like a whipped dog...

Harold Wilson

Day 224

INSULT a Day!

I don't want to spoil a pleasant
day by talking to you...

LAGOON BOOKS

Day 225

INSULT
a Day!

Oh no, not you again...

Day 226

INSULT a Day!

You're so ugly that when you joined an ugly contest, they said 'Sorry, no professionals'...

Day 227

INSULT a Day!

She was the kind of girl who'd eat all your cashews and leave you with nothing but peanuts and filberts...

Raymond Chandler

Day 228

LAGOON BOOKS

INSULT a Day!

Don't look out of the window,
people will think that it's Hallowe'en...

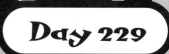

Day 229

INSULT a Day!

For two cents, I'd give you a piece of my mind - and all of yours...

LAGOON BOOKS

Day 230

INSULT a Day!

Mother Nature must really hate you because you remind her so much of all her mistakes!

Day 231

LAGOON BOOKS

INSULT a Day!

You've a face like a million dollars - all green and wrinkled...

LAGOON BOOKS

Day 232

Billy: My ideal woman has to have a
great sense of humor.
Jilly: That will have to be the only
sense she has.

Day 233

INSULT
a Day!

Boy: Where have you been all my life?
Girl: What do you mean - I wasn't even born for the first half of it?

Day 234

INSULT a Day!

You're the only person I know who failed their driving test for looking in the mirror too often...

Day 235

LAGOON BOOKS

INSULT a Day!

Boy: Would you like to come back to my place for a bacardi and grope?
Girl: Just a gin and platonic, please.

Day 236

LAGOON BOOKS

INSULT a Day!

You possess an intellect rivaled only by garden tools...

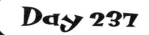

Day 237

INSULT

a Day!

Go jump off the world...

Day 238

INSULT a Day!

The common people swarm like common flies...

Shakespeare

Day 239

INSULT a Day!

You must be an experiment in Artificial Stupidity...

Day 240

INSULT
a Day!

She's the kind of woman who climbed the ladder of success -
wrong by wrong...

Mae West

Day 241

INSULT

a Day!

You really should stop buying material
for your dresses at curtain sales...

Day 242

LAGOON BOOKS

INSULT a Day!

She thought she was getting a model husband - but he's not a working model...

Day 244

LAGOON BOOKS

INSULT a Day!

She's got such a narrow mind, when she walks fast her earrings bang together...

John Cantu

Day 245

LAGOON BOOKS

INSULT

a Day!

That's a nice suit you're wearing.
When did the clown die?

Day 246

INSULT
a Day!

Mary: You've got a smile that could light up a whole town.

Martin: You've got a mouth that could accommodate a whole town...

Day 247

LAGOON BOOKS

INSULT
a Day!

Boy: What time would you like me to set the alarm for in the morning?

Girl: I don't care. My boyfriend always gets me up.

Day 248

INSULT
a Day!

You take your troubles like a man -
you blame them on a woman...

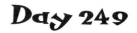

Day 249

INSULT
a Day!

You're so dumb, you would put lipstick
on your forehead in order to
make-up your mind...

Day 250

INSULT
a Day!

Annie: If we went on a date, how would you describe me to your friends?
Barry: If I was desperate enough to date you, I wouldn't have any friends...

LAGOON BOOKS

Day 251

INSULT a Day!

Some folks seem to have descended
from the chimpanzee later
than others...

Kin Hubbard

LAGOON
BOOKS

Day 252

INSULT
a Day!

It's people like you who give scum a bad name...

Day 253

LAGOON BOOKS

INSULT
a Day!

You're so ugly that if you look out the window you get arrested for mooning...

Day 254

LAGOON BOOKS

INSULT
a Day!

You are the sort of person people
emigrate to avoid...

Day 255

LAGOON BOOKS

INSULT a Day!

Boris: Excuse me, were you looking at me just then?

Doris: Yes, I thought from a distance you were good looking. Sorry, I forgot my glasses...

Day 256

INSULT a Day!

I heard you got a brain transplant and the brain rejected you...

Day 257

INSULT a Day!

You've got more chins than the Hong Kong telephone book...

Day 258

LAGOON BOOKS

INSULT

a Day!

Don't you have a home to go to?

LAGOON BOOKS

Day 259

INSULT
a Day!

You have a face like a
Saint-Bernard...

Day 260

LAGOON BOOKS

INSULT
a Day!

Sit down and give your mind a rest...

Day 261

LAGOON BOOKS

INSULT a Day!

Be careful when reading health books;
you may die of a misprint...

Mark Twain

Day 262

INSULT a Day!

Bill: Don't go away - I'm just going to put the kettle on.
Jill: Are you sure it will fit you?

Day 263

LAGOON BOOKS

INSULT a Day!

Shane: When can we be alone?
Sheila: When we're not with each other...

Day 264

INSULT
a Day!

Underneath your flabby exterior is an enormous lack of character...

Day 265

LAGOON BOOKS

INSULT a Day!

Lance: What's your number, I'd love to take you on a date?

Lucy: It's in the phone book...

Day 266

LAGOON BOOKS

INSULT a Day!

Oh my God, look at you.
Was anyone else hurt in the accident?

Day 267

INSULT a Day!

You have very striking features. How often exactly have you been struck?

Day 268

LAGOON BOOKS

Insult a Day!

Some folks are wise and some
are otherwise...

Tobias George Smolett

Day 269

LAGOON BOOKS

INSULT a Day!

I don't respond to losers...

Day 270

LAGOON BOOKS

INSULT
a Day!

Martin: Can I buy you a drink?
Martha: I'd rather just have the cash...

Day 272

LAGOON
BOOKS

INSULT
a Day!

Don't feel bad - a lot of people have no talent, and you're most of them...

Day 273

INSULT a Day!

I reprimanded my brother for
mimicking you.
I told him not to act like a fool...

Day 274

INSULT

a Day!

Boy: What's a girl like you doing in a
nice place like this?
Girl: Trying to avoid you...

Day 275

INSULT
a Day!

You're so fat, when you walked in front of the TV I missed 3 commercials...

Day 276

INSULT
a Day!

His mother should have thrown him
away and kept the stork...

Mae West

Day 277

INSULT
a Day!

Where I come from they shoot
people like you...

Day 278

LAGOON
BOOKS

INSULT a Day!

May your spouse agree with your mother-in-law about EVERYTHING...

LAGOON BOOKS

Day 279

INSULT

a Day!

You certainly fell out of the ugly tree, and it looks like you hit every branch on the way down...

Day 280

INSULT a Day!

Boy: I love you.
Girl: I love chocolate, but I wouldn't bother chatting it up...

Day 281

INSULT
a Day!

Bill: I'd like to take you to dinner.
Jill: Sure - can you pick me up again afterwards?

Day 282

Insult a Day!

I don't want you to turn the other cheek - it's just as ugly...

Day 283

LAGOON BOOKS

INSULT a Day!

A $400 suit on him would look like
socks on a rooster...

Earl Long

Day 284

INSULT a Day!

I bet your brain feels as good as new, seeing that you've never used it...

Day 285

INSULT
a Day!

I'm already visualizing the duct tape over your mouth...

Day 287

LAGOON BOOKS

LAGOON
BOOKS

INSULT
a Day!

You couldn't get a job as a
firing squad target...

Day 288

Barry: Shall we go all the way?
Mary: Yes, as long as it's in different directions...

INSULT a Day!

Every person has the right to be ugly, but you're abusing the privilege...

Day 290

INSULT
a Day!

Johnny: When should I phone you?
Jilly: Whenever I'm not there.

LAGOON BOOKS

Day 291

INSULT
a Day!

You have double chins all the way
down to your stomach...

Mark Twain

LAGOON
BOOKS

Day 292

a Day!

Girl: When will we meet again?
Boy: In another life, I hope...

Day 293

INSULT a Day!

Never trust a man with short legs - his brain's too near his butt...

Day 294

INSULT

a Day!

The primates claim you were a throwback...

Day 295

LAGOON BOOKS

INSULT
a Day!

You have not a single
redeeming defect...

Day 296

LAGOON BOOKS

INSULT
a Day!

You're so ugly when you go to the beautician it would take 12 hours - for a quote!

Day 297

LAGOON BOOKS

Insult a Day!

You got your brain very early.
Apparently the warranty has run out...

Day 298

INSULT
a Day!

LAGOON
BOOKS

I like long walks, especially when they are taken by people who annoy me...

Fred Allen

Day 299

INSULT a Day!

I like that outfit you're wearing. You should hang on to it - it'll come back in style some day...

LAGOON BOOKS

Day 300

INSULT
a Day!

He's so dumb he can't fart and chew gum at the same time...

Day 301

LAGOON BOOKS

INSULT
a Day!

You have the popularity of
bubonic plague...

Day 302

LAGOON
BOOKS

INSULT

a Day!

Why don't you go and get lost
somewhere where they have
no 'found' department?

Day 303

INSULT a Day!

You're so ugly you would make an onion cry...

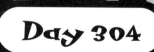

Day 304

LAGOON BOOKS

INSULT

a Day!

Women want mediocre men, and men are working hard to become as mediocre as possible...

Margaret Mead

Day 305

INSULT
a Day!

Why don't you take a vacation -
say, for about ten years?

LAGOON
BOOKS

Day 306

INSULT a Day!

Nice outfit, are you wearing it for a bet?

Day 307

LAGOON BOOKS

INSULT a Day!

You're so ugly your mom had to be drunk to breast feed you...

Day 308

LAGOON BOOKS

INSULT a Day!

When they were giving out brains, you should have asked for one to go...

Day 310

INSULT
a Day!

If I looked as bad as you do I'd wear a mask...

Day 311

INSULT
a Day!

He could never see a belt without
hitting below it...

Margot Asquith

Day 313

LAGOON BOOKS

INSULT

a Day!

Why don't you stick your head out the window - feet first?

LAGOON BOOKS

Day 314

INSULT a Day!

Peter: I'm a photographer for a model agency:
I've been looking for a face like yours.

Petra: I'm a plastic surgeon. I've been looking
for a face like yours.

Day 315

INSULT a Day!

Why don't you resign from the human race?

Day 316

INSULT

a Day!

It's nice to see you - but next time,
just send a postcard...

Day 317

LAGOON
BOOKS

INSULT a Day!

I feel so miserable without you; it's almost like having you here...

Stephen Bishop

Day 318

INSULT a Day!

It was nice of you to come.
When are you going?

Day 319

LAGOON BOOKS

LAGOON
BOOKS

INSULT
a Day!

Men are like car alarms. They both make a lot of noise no one listens to...

Diana Jordan

Day 320

INSULT
a Day!

Boy: Do I get the impression that you're
playing hard to get?
Girl: No, I'm playing impossible to get...

Day 321

LAGOON BOOKS

INSULT a Day!

You were one of the first to get a brain, before they were perfected...

Day 322

LAGOON BOOKS

INSULT a Day!

Keep talking, someday you'll say something intelligent...

Day 323

LAGOON BOOKS

INSULT
a Day!

Some day you will find yourself -
and wish you hadn't...

Day 324

LAGOON BOOKS

INSULT a Day!

Why don't you start neglecting your appearance? Maybe it'll go away...

Day 325

LAGOON BOOKS

INSULT a Day!

LAGOON BOOKS

He's opposite to humanity...

Shakespeare

Day 328

INSULT
a Day!

You should do some soul-searching.
Maybe you'll find one...

Day 329

LAGOON BOOKS

INSULT a Day!

He ought to take a closer look at his family tree.
There must have been a lot of lemons...

Day 330

a Day!

I don't know what makes you so dumb but it really works...

Day 331

LAGOON BOOKS

INSULT a Day!

Hey buddy, that's a nice shirt, what brand is it? Clearance?

Day 332

INSULT a Day!

Girl: What do you think of the music here?

Boy: Better than the company...

Day 333

INSULT a Day!

You're so ugly they didn't give you a costume when you tried out for *Star Wars*...

Day 334

INSULT a Day!

I've just learned about his illness.
Let's hope it's nothing trivial...

Irvin S. Cobb

Day 335

INSULT a Day!

She's got the kind of heart that's best
kept in cold storage...

Day 336

LAGOON BOOKS

INSULT
a Day!

Is your family happy, or do you go
home at night?

Day 338

INSULT a Day!

She's so boring you fall asleep
halfway through her name...

Alan Bennett

LAGOON
BOOKS

Day 339

INSULT
a Day!

You always find yourself lost in thought - it's an unfamiliar territory...

Day 341

LAGOON BOOKS

INSULT
a Day!

Next time you cook with gas,
inhale some...

Day 343

INSULT
a Day!

If I've said anything to offend you,
I meant it...

Day 344

LAGOON BOOKS

INSULT
a Day!

She is too mean to have her name repeated...

Shakespeare

Day 345

LAGOON
BOOKS

INSULT a Day!

Boris: You must tell me your name.
Doris: It begins with 'Mrs'. Shall I
bother to continue?

Day 346

INSULT
a Day!

He was one of those men who possess almost every gift, except the gift of the power to use them...

Charles Kingsley

Day 347

INSULT
a Day!

I'd like to help you out.
Which way did you come in?

Day 349

LAGOON
BOOKS

INSULT
a Day!

Brains aren't everything. In fact in
your case they're nothing...

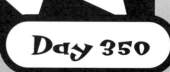

Day 350

LAGOON
BOOKS

INSULT a Day!

LAGOON BOOKS

You couldn't tell if she was dressed for an opera or an operation...

Irvin S. Cobb

Day 351

Boy: Can I have your name?
Girl: Why - haven't you already got one?

Day 352

INSULT a Day!

Do you ever wonder what life would be like if you'd had enough oxygen at birth?

Day 353

INSULT a Day!

Girl: You remind me of the last person I went out with.
Boy: That must be going back a bit...

Day 354

INSULT
a Day!

Did your parents ever ask you to run away from home?

Day 355

LAGOON BOOKS

INSULT
a Day!

What a brazen-fac'd varlet art thou...

Shakespeare

Day 356

INSULT
a Day!

Are you always this stupid or are you making a special effort today?

Day 357

INSULT a Day!

I can always tell when you are lying.
Your lips move...

Day 358

LAGOON BOOKS

INSULT a Day!

There was something about you that I liked, but you spent it...

Day 359

INSULT a Day!

I believe in respect for the dead; in fact,
I might be able to respect you if you
WERE dead...

Day 361

LAGOON BOOKS

INSULT a Day!

You're so stupid you would buy a solar-powered flashlight...

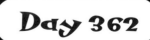

Day 362

INSULT
a Day!

Don't worry about trying to get rid of that halitosis - you'll always be unpopular anyway...

LAGOON BOOKS

Day 363

INSULT a Day!

I will always love the false image
I had of you...

Ashleigh Brilliant

Day 364

LAGOON BOOKS

INSULT
a Day!

The only way he can hear any good about himself is to talk to himself...

Day 365